I0190670

# The Law is not a Curse:
# Paul's Midrash in Galatians
# Workbook

*An in-depth study of Galatians that recovers the ancient worldview and its use of language*

## Dr. Anne K. Davis

**BibleInteract**
UNCOVERING THE MYSTERIES OF THE KINGDOM OF GOD

This edition © 2013 by Anne Davis. All rights reserved. No part of this publication may be reproduced or transmitted in any form or by any means without permission of the publisher.

All Scripture quotations, unless otherwise noted, are taken from the *New American Standard Bible*®, Copyright © 1960, 1962, 1963, 1968, 1971, 1972, 1973, 1975, 1977, 1995 by The Lockman Foundation Used by permission. (www.Lockman.org)

*The NASB uses italics to indicate words that have been added for clarification. Citations are shown with small capital letters.*

*NT is an abbreviation for New Testament; HS is an abbreviation for Hebraic Scriptures, that is, the Old Testament.*

Published by BibleInteract
ISBN-13: 978-0615773728
ISBN-10: 0615773729

BibleInteract
865 Los Pueblos Street
Los Alamos, NM 87544

www.bibleinteract.com

# Author's Note

The purpose of the book, *The Law is not a Curse: Paul's Midrash in Galatians,* is to acquaint you with Paul's ancient methods of searching the Hebrew Scriptures, which unveiled deep meaning to guide Christian believers in Galatia who were facing a serious crisis. In each chapter of this workbook you will:

- Review the purpose of the chapter
- Define important words and concepts
- Answer questions to assess your comprehension
- Actively enter into discussion with your peers, which will require advanced skills of analysis, comparison, organized thought, an ability to support an argument, and application.
- Practice a unique skill that will improve and facilitate your methods of Bible study.
- Consider ways to apply what you have learned to a life of faith in Christ.

# TABLE OF CONTENTS

# Introduction

## Getting Started and Suggestions for Group Leaders

### Leading a Discussion

Despite all that has been written about Paul's Letter to the Galatians, you will undoubtedly find this book filled with new information that will be challenging and provocative. If you are a teacher or group leader, you will need to read the entire book first to understand Paul's first century methods of interpreting the Hebrew Scriptures and the depth of meaning that results. To master all that the book offers will necessitate more than a quick read. However, after what will undoubtedly be considerable work on your part, you will be able to help others understand how Paul penetrates the depth of Scripture and how others can appreciate the remarkable disclosures he uncovers. Even more important, with the assistance of the Workbook, you will be promoting lively discussion, stimulating incisive questions, and encouraging a search in the Scriptures for meaningful answers.

Let me make a comment on the name of God's son. I have used the name Yeshua in this Workbook because the focus of the book is to encourage you to think with a first century Hebraic mind. However, you should use the name that is most comfortable to your group. If they prefer the name Yeshua, then that is the name that you should use.

### Considering New Ideas

I will now follow my own advice by asking a provocative question that, I trust, will promote lively discussion (or at least thoughtful consideration). Why is it important to understand Paul's ancient methods of exegesis in Galatians instead of simply reading the letter for what it says on the surface? You can certainly follow the simple path if you choose. However, you will then miss the drama of Paul's agonizing struggle to dislodge Jewish believers in Christ from the comfort of their traditional religious beliefs. Furthermore if you, like many of the original recipients of Paul's letter, remain locked in your dogma, then you will likely miss the extraordinary new understanding that Paul has found in the Hebrew Scriptures and that he saw verified by experiences in his midst. You will remain in your comfortable tradition about such troubling concepts as "works of the law," "curse of the law," and "cast out the slave woman" (Paul claims that Hagar, the slave woman, allegorically represents the children of Israel). The goal of this book is to encourage you to "wrestle with the text," and to draw your own conclusions after asking your own provocative questions. This Workbook will help you acquire the skills to answer your questions.

As the book leads you to consider Paul's methods of interpretation, you will realize that Paul's words are still working today to dislodge us from the comfort of our own religious ideas. By failing to recognize and understand Paul's ancient methods of searching the Hebrew Scriptures, we have missed the depth of what he is trying to tell us. That depth not only explains *how* God is fulfilling His "promise of the Spirit" but also tells us *how* we can live in the promise of the Spirit. But first, we must understand and follow what Paul is trying to tell us.

## The Workbook

The Workbook contains Questions for Comprehension, which assess an understanding of the chapter. However, these Questions for Comprehension can also be an opportunity for the discussion leader to review the main ideas of the chapter before proceeding to the more penetrating Questions for Discussion. If you are a group leader, you may wish to ask the group first if they had trouble with any of the questions. Then we suggest that you prepare to lead a discussion on just one of the Comprehension Questions that you think might be helpful to the group.

The purpose of Questions for Discussion is not only to consider ideas and thoughts that might be new, challenging and provocative, but also to discuss how the information can be applied to one's life. Feel free to create and add your own Questions for Discussion. In fact, you might ask the students to compose one or more of their own questions for discussion before coming together as a group.

Digging Deeper has been designed with more challenging discussion questions. Depending on the level of your group, you may decide to skip these Digging Deeper questions altogether. Or, if you have a more advanced group, you may wish to delete some of the Discussion Questions in order to place more emphasis on Digging Deeper.

The Development of Bible Study Skills is an essential part of the Workbook, so don't pass over them too quickly. These study skills are designed not only to help the student search the Scriptures but also to build analytical and presentation skills. One of my students observed, regarding the exercises associated with these study skills, "This is teaching me how to think."

The Application Questions appear at the end of each chapter's activities but are perhaps one of the most important sections of the Workbook. These Application Questions should not be taken lightly nor should they be addressed quickly. It is important to complete the preceding work, which will undoubtedly be quite challenging, before proceeding to the Application Questions. Feel free to add your own Application Questions. You may also wish to request that each member of the group contribute his or her own application question for discussion as well.

## Leading a Discussion

By presenting a new perspective on Galatians (and likely new information and interpretive conclusions as well), I have chosen to intentionally encourage questions that lead not to definitive answers from the teacher but to provocative discussion. Students should eventually feel comfortable disputing the interpretive suggestions of the book's author and even of the discussion leader and other students. However, as a discussion leader you should guide the students to follow two important requirements.

First, the student should clearly and briefly state his or her main idea, which must then be followed by supporting evidence. The Bible study skill in Chapter 5 of the Workbook is "Building an Argument." Before arriving at Chapter 5, however, students will start to form a foundation in the first three chapters that will help them feel comfortable searching the Scriptures for what should prompt their questions, suggest possible answers, and provide supporting evidence. Chapter 4 introduces the analytical skill of handling that evidence responsibly, and Chapter 5 brings all the skills together for building a responsible presentation of an interpretation.

Second, the discussion leader should encourage the students to speak in a compassionate manner. The modern literary term for this rhetorical skill is "couching," which evokes a visual image of a psychiatrist speaking compassionately to a patient on the couch. The good doctor wishes his or her patient to confront some aspect of thinking that might best be changed to a more advantageous perspective. The group should also avoid direct confrontation. Try not to be judgmental. Instead, mimic our psychiatrist who gently employs couching terms.

- "Have you ever considered…?"
- "Perhaps there might be another possibility…"
- "For the sake of discussion, let us look at…"
- "I used to think that too, but now…"
- "There might be another way of approaching this verse…"

The goal of the book is not to dislodge students from the doctrinal belief systems and theologies with which they have been raised (although, in all fairness, a questioning approach does not rule out this possibility). Instead, you will discover in Chapter 3 that I encourage the reader to examine a brief overview of different broad theological positions. This consideration of other interpretive traditions should prompt discussion. The group leader should foster a compassionate desire by the students to understand the beliefs of others and to pursue a thoughtful explanation of one's own theology that is supported by evidence from Scripture.

There is another reason for encouraging the discussion of different positions. Before confronting any new interpretive suggestion, which this book will certainly stimulate, an essential prerequisite is to be solidly grounded in one's own belief system. There must be something solid against which we can responsibly consider and compare a new proposal. Furthermore, I tell my students that the book, *The Law is not a Curse: Paul's Midrash in Galatians,* may well be compatible, in some parts, with what they have already been taught. However, the book and the first century methods it employs will most certainly take them deeper in their understanding of Galatians in particular and in all of Scripture as well. A deeper understanding of what Paul calls "the promise of the Spirit" is often the "bait" that generates their excited expectation.

## Seeking Help

If you are unable to find answers and solutions to your own satisfaction, we have two suggestions. First, go to http://drannedavis.com and browse through the Frequently Asked Questions. You may find your answer there. You may also post your own question and we will do our best to respond as quickly as possible.

If you are a registered student in The Bible Learning University, an online educational program offered by BibleInteract, then you will have an Advisor who is qualified to answer your questions. For more information about The Bible Learning University, visit http://www.bibleinteract.com.

# Chapter 1

## The Opening Scene: Paul's Early Life

### Purpose

This chapter serves as an introduction to Paul's artistic use of language and his methods of midrash by encouraging you to identify with Paul in his early life as a Christian. Paul responded to crises in his own life by searching the Scriptures and seeking God's direction, which is the underlying principle of midrash.

In the Scriptures, the text conveys more than a simple story. Instead, the narrative is teeming with artistic language that leads us to depth of meaning. The Holy Writings are where God makes Himself known, not in the Greek, western way of simply relating an event in a clear, well developed, analytical manner. Scripture, on the other hand, is like an onion with multiple layers. It is like a bank of fog where we cannot see things clearly until we walk into the unknown mist. So, in this session you will apply your new ability to "listen to the text" in order to penetrate beyond the outer layer of the story to its inner, mysterious elements.

### Definitions

When reading the chapter it is important to note and understand important terms and concepts. Listed below are several in Chapter 1 that you may wish to define.

1. Methods of Midrash

2. Saul

3. Irony

4. Sanhedrin

5. Nabateans

6. Beit Midrash

_____
_____

7. Gamaliel

_____
_____

8. Barnabus

_____
_____

## Questions for Comprehension

How well did you understand the chapter? First try answering these questions on your own to the greatest extent possible before reviewing them in your study group. You may be surprised by the various nuances that different people have perceived. Even though the questions are designed to assess how well you understand Chapter 1, there is nevertheless a depth of understanding to each question or exercise.

1. Describe the various crises that Paul faced in Damascus. How did he respond? Be as specific as possible.

_____
_____
_____
_____
_____
_____
_____
_____
_____
_____
_____
_____
_____

## Developing Bible Study Skills

**Imagine the Land through an Historical Atlas**

To make the story of Paul come alive in your imagination you will need a sense of the land. There are numerous historical atlases of Bible times which not only offer topographical maps and historical background but also explain specific historical events during different periods of history in ancient Israel. Refer to the Recommended Reading List at the end of Chapter 1 for a suggested Bible atlas.

_Locate on a map of the ancient Roman world the cities of Jerusalem, Damascus, Caesarea, Tarsus and Antioch. Why was sea travel from Caesarea to Tarsus preferable to an overland journey?_

✝

_On a map of the ancient Roman world, identify the topographical features between Jerusalem and Damascus. What would have been Paul's most likely route between these two cities?_

✝

_Paul declares that he was a Benjamite. Locate the geographic areas where the twelve tribes of Israel settled after they entered the land of Israel. How did the location of the tribe of Benjamin affect its subsequent historical development? Consider in particular the time of the divided monarchy and the period of the Roman occupation._

2. Why and how did Paul's return to Tarsus present a crisis in his life? How did he respond? Be as specific as possible.

3. Explain how Tarsus, the city in which Paul was raised, had an impact on his life and helped mold his character.

4. Describe the contrast and tension between Ananias, a Christian who was living in Damascus, and Paul the new Christian believer. How do you think Paul attempted to relieve this tension?

5. In Galatians 1:15, how does Paul suggest a similar incident that we see in Jeremiah 1:5? Paul alludes to the HS frequently. How can you identify an allusion in the NT to a verse or passage in the HS?

## Questions for Discussion

There may not be a "right" or "wrong" answer to these discussion questions since they are designed for discussion. However, you should practice stating your main idea as a sound thesis and then supporting your view by substantial biblical evidence. If you speak from a traditional standpoint, be prepared to support it with evidence. Try to avoid speaking only from tradition.

1. Read the account of Elijah in 1 Kings 19:1-15. Compare this passage with Galatians 1:17.

**1 Kings 19:1-15**

*Now Ahab told Jezebel all that Elijah had done, and how he had killed all the prophets with the sword. $^2$ Then Jezebel sent a messenger to Elijah, saying, "So may the gods do to me and even more, if I do not make your life as the life of one of them by tomorrow about this time." $^3$ And he was afraid and arose and ran for his life and came to Beersheba, which belongs to Judah, and left his servant there. $^4$ But he himself went a day's journey into the wilderness, and came and sat down under a juniper tree; and he requested for himself that he might die, and said, "It is enough; now, O LORD, take my life, for I am not better than my fathers." $^5$ He lay down and slept under a juniper tree; and behold, there was an angel touching him, and he said to him, "Arise, eat." $^6$ Then he looked and behold, there was at his head a bread cake baked on hot stones, and a jar of water. So he ate and drank and lay down again. $^7$ The angel of the LORD came again a second time and touched him and said, "Arise, eat, because the journey is too great for you." $^8$ So he arose and ate and drank, and went in the strength of that food forty days and forty nights to Horeb, the mountain of God.*

*$^9$ Then he came there to a cave and lodged there; and behold, the word of the LORD came to him, and He said to him, "What are you doing here, Elijah?" $^{10}$ He said, "I have been very zealous for the LORD, the God of hosts; for the sons of Israel have forsaken Your covenant, torn down Your altars and killed Your prophets with the sword. And I alone am left; and they seek my life, to take it away."*

*$^{11}$ So He said, "Go forth and stand on the mountain before the LORD." And behold, the LORD was passing by! And a great and strong wind was rending the mountains and breaking in pieces the rocks before the LORD; but the LORD was not in the wind. And after the wind an earthquake, but the LORD was not in the earthquake. $^{12}$ After the earthquake a fire, but the LORD was not in the fire; and after the fire a sound of a gentle blowing. $^{13}$ When Elijah heard it, he wrapped his face in his mantle and went out and stood in the entrance of the cave. And behold, a voice came to him and said, "What are you doing here, Elijah?" $^{14}$ Then he said, "I have been very zealous for the LORD, the God of hosts; for the sons of Israel have forsaken Your covenant, torn down Your altars and killed Your prophets with the sword. And I alone am left; and they seek my life, to take it away."*

*$^{15}$ The LORD said to him, "Go, return on your way to the wilderness of Damascus, and when you have arrived, you shall anoint Hazael king over Aram*

**Galatians 1:11-17**

***Paul Defends His Ministry***
*$^{11}$ For I would have you know, brethren, that the gospel which was preached by me is not according to man. $^{12}$ For I neither received it from man, nor was I taught it, but I received it through a revelation of Yeshua Christ.*

*$^{13}$ For you have heard of my former manner of life in Judaism, how I used to persecute the church of God beyond measure and tried to destroy it; $^{14}$ and I was advancing in Judaism beyond many of my contemporaries among my countrymen, being more extremely zealous for my ancestral traditions. $^{15}$ But when God, who had set me apart even from my mother's womb and called me through His grace, was pleased $^{16}$ to reveal His Son in me so that I might preach Him among the Gentiles, I did not immediately consult with flesh and blood, $^{17}$ **nor did I go up to Jerusalem to those who were apostles before me; but I went away to Arabia, and returned once more to Damascus.***

2. How is Paul's journey an echo of Elijah? Do you think the relationship between the two passages is intentional? If so, why? If not, why not?

_____
_____
_____
_____
_____
_____
_____

3. Make a chart contrasting the differences between the Written Law and the Oral Law.

| Written Law | Oral Law |
|---|---|
|  |  |

4. How did Paul's training in a *beit midrash* contribute to his knowledge and understanding of the Oral Law as well as his use of methods that led to this body of Scriptural interpretation?

_____
_____
_____
_____
_____
_____
_____

## Application Questions

1. Did Yeshua ever use the Oral Law to make a point? For example, turn to the gospels in the NT to find and list the times he said "it is written" in contrast to "you have heard." In these passages, did Yeshua ever use the Oral Law to make a point?

_____
_____
_____
_____
_____
_____
_____
_____
_____

2. How and when has Scripture helped you through a crisis? Explain your answer.

_____
_____
_____
_____
_____
_____
_____
_____

*Digging Deeper*

Read Luke's account of Paul's first visit as a Christian to Jerusalem (Acts 9:26-30). Then compare this account in Acts with Paul's own words in Galatians (Gal. 1:18-24). What are the arguments for and against the reliability of each? Is it possible to harmonize the two accounts? Explain your answer.

❧

Imagine the 15 days that Peter, the fisherman, and Paul, the scholar, were engaged in intense discussion. Take the role of each and recreate the discussion. Then dialogue regarding the relevance of this exercise to today's world.

❧

What are various ways that people perceive Paul? Discuss three ways that the presentation differs from traditional teaching.

# Chapter 2

## Fast Forward: The Crisis in Galatia

### Purpose

This chapter is a continuing narrative that jumps forward in Paul's life to the crisis in Galatia. You may be surprised to learn how many interpretive possibilities exist. You will be challenged to identify your own traditional understanding about the nature of the crisis in Galatia, and you will discuss with your peers the source of this tradition as well as the nature of other competing interpretations.

### Definitions

1. Protagonist

2. Jerusalem Council

3. Central Galatian theory

4. Southern Galatian theory

5. Epistle

6. Chiasmus

7. Circumcision

8. *Kashrut*

9. Justification

10. Hyperbole

11. Pun

12. Rhetoric

## Questions for Comprehension

1. How does the beginning of Paul's letter to the Galatians deviate from epistolary tradition? Explain why these changes would have startled an ancient reader.

2. How are Jewish believers in Galatia the protagonists in this drama?

3. How does the literary technique of asking rhetorical questions operate? Explain the rhetorical nature of Paul's questions in Gal 3:1-5.

_____
_____
_____
_____
_____
_____
_____
_____
_____
_____

4. Describe the "false gospel."

_____
_____
_____
_____
_____
_____
_____
_____
_____
_____
_____

5. Use your Bible atlas to locate the two possible locations of Galatia (you may wish to coordinate information from the web with the map in your atlas). Then consider how each possible location of Galatia affects the resulting interpretation.

_____
_____
_____
_____
_____
_____
_____
_____
_____
_____
_____
_____
_____
_____

# Developing Bible Study Skills

### Finding a Source from the Recommended Readings

Your local library will probably not have the resources listed at the end of each chapter. Or if they do, they may not have all of them. Go to your local library and inquire about the Inter-Library Loan Program. Your librarian will explain how you can order books, articles and other source material suggested at the end of each chapter. Almost all libraries are now participants in the Inter-Library Loan Program, which sends materials by mail from other libraries around the country.

### All Books are Biased

All authors have perspectives based on their experience, educational training, family background and environment. Ask any journalist how many different accounts will be given by people who attend or witness the same event. There will probably be as many varieties of the re-telling as there are people to tell it. So, what should you do when reading source materials?

- Look to see if the author identifies his or her purpose and perspective when writing the book.
- Sometimes authors state assumptions that they bring to a written work.
- As you read, look for biases and underlying assumptions that the author may not have identified.
- Check the internet to learn more about the author.
- After reading a book or article, draw your own conclusions about the reputation and reliability of the author.

✠

*The subject of religion is especially prone to bias. One might argue that all ministers, preachers, priests and rabbis are influenced by their traditional doctrine and dogma. Explain and discuss this suggestion.*

✠

*Compare the different styles of presentation between* Paul: A Critical Life *by Jerome Murphy-O'Connor and* The Apostle: A Life of Paul *by John Pollock (both books are listed in the Recommended Reading in Chapter 1). What are the advantages and disadvantages of each style?*

✠

*Consider what you have read so far in* The Law is not a Curse. *Then rate the author, Dr. Anne Davis, by the five assessment suggestions above. You may wish to conduct this exercise again after you have completed Chapters 1-6.*

## Questions for Discussion

1. What did the "freedom group" believe and practice? How do their interpretive beliefs compare to traditions and denominations today?

2. If circumcision is the sign of God's covenant with His people Israel, then what has Christ accomplished to change and elevate the nature of that sign? How does the gift of the Holy Spirit elevate the sign of circumcision?

3. Argue from the two positions about the identity of the Jews in Galatia. First, support a claim that they were sincere Christian believers. Second, develop an argument with supporting evidence that the Jews in Galatia were either unbelievers or insincere Christians.

4. First explain your traditional understanding of the recipients of Paul's letter. Then, after considering the information in Chapter 2, who do you think were the Jews and who were the Gentiles? Support your position with both internal and external evidence (internal is from Scripture and external refers to all other kinds of evidence).

## Application Questions

1. Review Paul's use of sarcastic irony. Then find two examples in the Gospels where Yeshua uses irony directed against the Pharisees. In each case is it sarcasm or ridicule? How would the disciples have perceived this irony as humor? Compare your answers with your traditional understanding of Yeshua's conflict with the Pharisees before you completed Chapter 2 of this book.

2. Explain how the dissension in Galatia was a conflict between law and lawlessness. Is the same issue found among believers in Yeshua today?

3. We all have doctrinal belief systems. Are you willing to have those systems examined by Yeshua to see if they line up with the way he dealt with people in the first century? Give an example of a doctrinal belief system from your life experience.

## Digging Deeper

Identify two examples of discrepancies between Luke's account in Acts and Paul's own words in his epistles. Then discuss how you might explain these discrepancies.

❧

Define chiasmus. Then explain how Galatians 1:3-4 is composed in a chiastic structure. After you perceive the chiastic structure in these two verses, how does this understanding influence your interpretation?

❧

Play the role of Peter at Antioch regarding food laws. Then play the role of Paul.

# Chapter 3

## Confronting Tradition: Then and Now

### Purpose

You will be searching the Hebrew Scriptures to view its plain meaning about God's wonderful promises to the Gentile nations. As you examine the Scriptures, you will begin to understand the daunting challenge that Paul faced, for he needed to convince his Jewish contemporaries (and those Gentile believers who were studying the Law) about his exciting new discoveries from the Hebrew Scriptures. Paul's new understanding is going to unsettle the Galatian believers and force them to confront their long-established customs. You too have traditions that will undoubtedly be disturbed and challenged. Therefore, it is incumbent upon you, as it was also incumbent upon the Galatians, to recognize and acknowledge your own conventional understanding. Then, once you understand your own tradition, you can responsibly consider other suggestions. You will likely be confronting your tradition about Paul's Letter to the Galatians in general, and about Paul's phrase "works of the law" in particular.

### Definitions

You need to understand the following terms and concepts.

1. *Pistis*

2. Monolithic

3. Hellenistic

4. *Kashrut*

5. Gentiles

6. Linguistic

7. Literal

_____

_____

_____

8. Figurative

_____

_____

_____

## Questions for Comprehension

1. What is your traditional understanding of "works of the law?" Make a list of questions that this chapter is stimulating in your mind about Paul's use of the term "works of the law." How are you responding to these questions?

_____

_____

_____

_____

_____

_____

_____

_____

2. Briefly describe the Lutheran, Reformed and Catholic theologies. How has the more recent position originated by Stendahl and Sanders challenged these theologies?

_____

_____

_____

_____

_____

_____

_____

3. According to the Hebrew Scriptures, what are the basic usages of "work?" How does your answer relate to Paul's use of the term, "works of the law?"

_____

_____

_____

_____

_____

_____

_____

# Developing Bible Study Skills

### Searching the Scriptures

The artistic nature of the biblical language offers linguistic clues to guide the listener (or the reader in our modern world) back to the Scriptures to search for deeper meaning. In ancient times, written texts were scarce so memorization was the common method of instruction. Today we don't memorize Scripture, but we can use a concordance. Here are two suggestions of concordances that might be helpful.

1) *Young's Analytical Concordance to the Bible* by Robert Young is suitable for beginners because it includes part of the verse in which the search-word appears. Youngs also gives a transliteration of the original Hebrew (for the HS) and Greek (for the NT) rather than relying exclusively on the original language. Youngs is tied to the King James Version of the Bible.

2) *Zondervan NIV Exhaustive Concordance* is another good option for those who do not know the original languages. Zondervan's concordance is tied to the New International Version.

3) Those who know Greek and/or Hebrew should use a concordance tied to the original languages.

4) Several online interlinear Bibles also have a concordance including http://biblos.com and http://www.blueletterbible.org

*Use a concordance to browse through verses in the Torah (the first five books of the HS) that include the word "work." Do you agree with the suggestion in this chapter that there are three categories of the way "work" is used in these five biblical books? Support your answer.*

✝

*Krister Stendahl made a huge leap to counter traditional thinking about Paul, Paul's position on truth versus works, and the very nature of our understanding about Galatians. Read Stendahl's book, Paul Among Jews and Gentiles, pages 1-23. What are the main ideas in these pages that Stendahl was proposing in 1977? Why were these ideas so revolutionary? How do you think Stendahl's suggestions were received after publication of his book?*

✝

*When I first read Stendahl's book many years ago, someone had marked a swastika in ink on*

## Questions for Discussion

1. Think of specific people you know who lean toward each of the following traditions: Lutheran, Reformed, Catholic, and the new position initiated by Stendahl and Sanders. With which position are you most comfortable? Explain your answer.

2. What is your traditional view of the "law" as the word is used in the New Testament, especially in Galatians? What are the questions that you are now asking?

3. What do you think is the role of works in the life of a Christian believer? How does your answer reflect one (or possibly more) of the four theological positions?

## Application Questions

1. Review the suggestions that first appeared in the Purpose section above. "You too have traditions that will undoubtedly be disturbed and challenged. Therefore, it is incumbent upon you, as it was also incumbent upon the Galatians, that you recognize and acknowledge your own conventional understanding. Then, once you understand your own tradition, you can responsibly consider other suggestions. You will likely be confronting your tradition about Galatians in general and about Paul's phrase 'works of the law' in particular." Do you agree that it is important to thoroughly identify your own traditions? Explain your answer.

2. What IS your traditional understanding of Paul's letter to the Galatians in general, and of Paul's use of the term "works of the law" in particular?

_____

_____

_____

_____

_____

_____

3. How has Chapter 3 in *The Law is not a Curse* confronted your tradition?

_____

_____

_____

_____

_____

_____

4. You should not change your interpretive understanding of Galatians or Paul's use of the term "works of the law" too quickly. To do so would be to "jump on a bandwagon" without first applying analytical thinking and critical analysis. Instead, make a list of all the questions that the unsettling nature of new ideas has stimulated in your mind. Return to these questions periodically as you work through the book and workbook.

_____

_____

_____

_____

_____

_____

_____

*Digging Deeper*

Read in their context (that is, in relation to the surrounding passage) the following verses about God's promises to the Gentiles: Genesis 12:3; 22:18; 28:4; 35:11; 48:4. What do these verses mean to you as a believer in Christ? What do you think they meant to the new Gentile believers in Galatia?

# Chapter 4

## Elevating Tradition with Artistic Language

### Purpose

In this chapter you will begin to delve into the technical aspects of the artistic nature of the biblical language. With your developing ancient Hebraic way of thinking you should be starting to recognize patterns formed by such linguistic devices as repetition, contrast and chiasm. The list of recommended readings, which will expand your understanding, is somewhat lengthy. So, you may be tempted to take the quick and easy route of searching for supplementary information on the web. I do not wish to discourage your web research, but I offer words of advice and caution in "Developing Skills for Bible Study."

### Definitions

1. Bible version

2. Translation

3. Sarcasm

4. Ridicule

5. Torah

6. *Yarah*

## Questions for Comprehension

1. First read Galatians 2:15-16 silently. Then read these verses aloud emphasizing rhythm, which provokes emotion, by hesitating in some places and by increasing the volume of your voice in others. How would Jewish believers have responded emotionally? How would Gentile believers have responded? How would the freedom group have responded?

2. Identify two examples of Paul's use of irony in Gal 2:15-16. How does this irony affect the meaning of the passage?

3. Identify and describe the five linguistic devices that Paul uses in Gal 2:15-16. How do these devices affect the meaning of the passage?

4. Dr. Davis suggests that there are three patterns in Gal 2:15-21. First identify the three patterns. Then explain how she arrived at these conclusions.

5. How did Paul use different verb tenses in Gal 2:15-16 to convey a sense of meaning? What is the understanding that results?

_____

_____

_____

_____

_____

# Developing Bible Study Skills

**Use the Internet Responsibly**

Unless you are a graduate-level student, your main source of information will likely become the internet. However, keep in mind that anyone can post anything. You will need to assess the reputation and reliability of each site you visit as follows:

1.  START by asking yourself, "What am I looking for?" Answer this question slowly, deliberately and carefully.
2.  ANALYZE THE SITE
    - Examine the leaders of the website. Do they have a particular slant or bias? Is the site trying to manipulate you to form certain conclusions?
    - Who created the site and why? What is the purpose of the site and what is it trying to accomplish?
    - Is the site personal (i.e. authored by an individual)? Or is the site sponsored by the government, or by an academic or some other institution?
    - How is the site funded? By sales? Contributions? Sponsorships?
    - Is there a way to contact a real person?
3.  ASSESS THE RELIABILITY
    - What is the reputation of the author and/or sponsor of the site?
    - Is the purpose of the site to inform, persuade or sell?
    - What is the accuracy of the site? Poor spelling and grammar is an indication of poor attention to details.
    - Is the site current or is it stale? When were the pages last revised?
    - What is the reliability of links to other sites?

_Identify three websites that offer Bible study online (you may wish to consider www.bibleinteract.tv). Start by asking, "What am I looking for?" Then follow the steps explained above to analyze the site and to assess its reliability. Discuss your findings in your study group._

✚

_Use the Internet to learn more about irony in Scripture. This linguistic device is rarely recognized, but is an important aspect of scriptural meaning. Select reliable sites for your information. Make a list of meaningful information you find._

## Questions for Discussion

1.  What has been your traditional understanding about "works of the law" in Gal 2:15-21? How does your interpretation compare with the information in this Chapter 4?

2.  Follow the suggestions under "Artistic Patterns in Gal 2:15-16" that you will find in the paragraph on pages 78-79. Start by re-reading these two verses without stopping and consider your traditional understanding. Next read Gal. 2:15-16 out loud. But this time *listen* for Paul's biting irony, the cacophony of repetition, and the clash of contrast. Finally, read these verses aloud one more time. Let the cadence of the sounds rise and fall as you produce the rhythm of the passage. Explain how you have recreated the likely scenario in Galatia when Paul's letter was read to the Galatian believers. How would this oral reading have affected the Galatians?

3.  How does the chiastic pattern in Gal 2:17-18 evoke an emotional response?

4.  How does the chiastic pattern in Gal 2:19-21 disturb the traditional thinking of Jewish Christians in Galatia? How does it disturb your own tradition of doctrine and dogma?

5. Review all the charts in Chapter 4. Practice explaining them to the members of your study group.

## Application Questions

1. If Christ lives in you, how does this affect the way you understand Scripture, both the Old and the New Testaments?

2. The Pharisee Paul had to get away with God for three years to sort out his doctrines and dogmas. Define doctrine. Define dogma. What is the distinction between the two? What is an example of your own doctrine? What is an example of your own dogma?

3. What doctrines have you adjusted in your maturing walk with Yeshua?

4. Dr. Davis states, *"One dies to the law by replacing its tedious study with faith in Christ, which permits one to truly live for God."* Does this mean that the Christian Bible should only be, or primarily be, the New Testament? Do NT believers need to know the Hebrew Scriptures? How would you explain your answer to a fellow believer? How would you explain your answer to a non-believer?

## Digging Deeper

How is the presentation in this chapter biased? That is, what preconceptions does the author bring to the viewpoint she has expressed? Do you agree with her preconceived assumptions?

∞

How has Galatians 2:15-16 become entrenched in Christian theology?

∞

How does an understanding of Paul's sarcasm change your thoughts about Gal. 2:15-16?

∞

An analogy in Scripture typically involves the relationship between two verses. The Book of Psalms is filled with analogies because it uses parallel lines that are related in some way, such as similarity, contrast, expansion or deletion. Turn to Psalm 15. Identify the parallel lines, and then consider the relationship between them. How do these analogies affect the meaning of the psalm?

# Chapter 5

## Uncovering Veiled Meaning from Scripture: Legal Midrash in Gal 3:6-9

### Purpose

After working diligently to understand Paul's artistic use of language, we turn now to the logic of Hebraic reasoning in legal midrash, which is quite different from western analytical thought. At this point, you should feel more comfortable with lively and provocative discussion with your peers than you did at the beginning of this book. However, there are two important criteria to consider in any discussion. First, you should listen patiently to the thoughts of others and seriously consider their suggestions. Second, you should insist that others present relevant supporting evidence from Scripture, which means that you must learn to give evidence as an example to others. Therefore, we will now be practicing how to develop a convincing argument.

### Definitions

1. Logic




2. Analogy




3. Proof-text




4. Exegesis




5. Syllogism




6. Dialectic




7. Rhetoric

8. Artistic Midrash

_____
_____
_____

9. Legal Midrash

_____
_____
_____

## Questions for Comprehension

1. Why does Dr. Davis call halachic midrash "legal midrash?"

_____
_____
_____
_____
_____
_____
_____

2. Create a chart that lists characteristics of legal midrash in one column and characteristics of Paul's artistic use of words in another column. Looking down the column of legal midrash, explain what legal midrash is. Then, looking down the other column, explain Paul's artistic use of words. Finally, compare the two columns to explain how legal midrash is different from Paul's artistic use of language.

| Legal Midrash | Paul's Artistic Use of Words |
|---|---|
|  |  |

3. What was the situation in Galatia that prompted Paul to explain his new discoveries from Scripture in Galatians 3:6-9?

4. Explain the additional analogical method of legal reasoning (not listed in Rabbi Ishmael's thirteen canons but used frequently in the Talmud), which Paul used in Gal 3:6-9.

5. Paul cites Genesis 15:16 and Genesis 12:3 in a construction of legal midrash. How are these two verses legally and conceptually similar?

6. What is a "deduction"? How is Galatians 3:8 a deduction in Paul's legal argument from Scripture?

7. How does Paul's method of legal midrash, which forms an analogy between Genesis 15:6 and Genesis 12:3, explain how God has fulfilled His promise to bless the Gentiles?

# Developing Bible Study Skills

### Building an Argument

- *Main Idea*: Start with your main idea, which will be the conclusion you have drawn after you searched the Scriptures. State your main idea briefly, simply and clearly.
- *Assumptions*: Explain any assumptions you bring to your argument. For example, you might say, "I am viewing Scripture as inspired by God because that would have been the perception at the time of Paul." Yet here is a word of caution. You will have to think carefully about any assumptions you bring from your tradition. Assumptions are acceptable, but they need to be stated as a preface to your argument.
- *Evidence from Scripture*: List your supporting evidence from Scripture. This internal evidence should take precedence over any external evidence.
- *External evidence*: You may add such external evidence as archaeological discoveries and/or ancient extra-biblical texts such as the Dead Sea Scrolls. However, an exposition by any author written after the ancient period of biblical composition is no longer primary evidence, which dates to the period of the biblical events, but secondary evidence, which is interpretation.
- *Conclusion*: End with a brief summary of your argument.

A paragraph typically starts with a topic sentence, which is the main idea of the paragraph. The remainder of the paragraph develops and supports the main idea in the topic sentence. Therefore, constructing a paragraph is a good way to practice building an argument. To further develop your skills, complete the following exercises on a separate sheet of paper.

*Complete a paragraph using the sentence below as your topic sentence. Build an argument that proves and supports this topic sentence. "The blessing of Abraham has come to the Gentiles."*

✠

*Consider the list of details below and compose one topic sentence that captures the main idea of these three details.*
- *Paul studied in a beit midrash.*
- *Ananias found Paul.*
- *Paul spoke in the synagogue in Damascus*

✠

*Construct a written argument on your own. Begin by selecting one of the following and make it the title of your paper. Then support this main idea with convincing evidence with well organized paragraphs.*
- *The Christian tradition has misunderstood Paul.*
- *Paul's artistic use of language influences the interpretation.*
- *Paul's use of the term "works of the law" has been misunderstood.*

## Questions for Discussion

1. Dr. Davis insists that nowhere in the Hebrew Scriptures can you find that God would justify the Gentiles by faith. Do you agree? Explain your answer.

2. Review the two theologies of dispensationalism and covenant theology. Which one makes you feel more comfortable? Explain your answer.

3. What is your traditional understanding of Galatians 3:6-9? Compare your traditional understanding with the explanation in this Chapter 5. Which of the two do you believe is more valid? Why? Explain your answer.

## Application Questions

1. What is a miracle that you have experienced? How has this miracle changed your life?

2. Do we need to wait for a dramatic miracle to see the hand of God? Explain your answer.

_____
_____
_____
_____
_____
_____
_____
_____

3. In the last three days, what have you seen and experienced that is the hand of God?

_____
_____
_____
_____
_____
_____
_____
_____
_____
_____

## Digging Deeper

Use the web responsibly (by following the steps listed in the last Chapter 4) to learn more about Dispensationalism, which is a theology characteristic of the Protestant evangelical movement as well as some other mainline Protestant denominations. Select someone who knows little or nothing about Dispensationalism and explain this theology to that person.

❧

Follow the same steps described in the exercise above, but this time with Covenant Theology. Select someone who knows little or nothing about these theologies, and explain them by comparing Covenant Theology and Dispensationalism.

❧

Consider the question, "What is Paul trying to say about Abraham in Galatians 3:6-9?" Search the Scriptures to understand the answer from Scripture. Then build two arguments. The first will be the answer from your tradition (with supporting evidence). The second will be the answer as explained in Chapter 5 (again with supporting evidence).

# Chapter 6

## Solving Problems of Interpretation: Paul's Method of Legal Reasoning

### Purpose

Chapter 5 gave you much introductory information to help you understand the Hebraic concept of legal midrash, which searches the Hebrew Scriptures for deep and veiled meaning. At the end of the last chapter, you saw one simple example of legal midrash in Galatians 3-9. You are now ready to tackle Galatians 3:10-13, which is an intricate construction of two separate, but related, legal arguments from the Hebrew Scriptures. The final conclusion from all of Paul's legal midrash, which starts in Galatians 3:6, appears in Galatians 3:14. This conclusion may seem powerful at first to those who do not understand the legal midrash that leads to it. However, when you understand the legal midrash, the conclusion becomes no less than breathtaking.

### Definitions

1. Analogical

2. Antithesis

3. Deduction

4. Enigmatic

5. Explicative

6. Gamaliel the Elder

7. Hillel

_____
_____
_____

8. Logical Interpretation

_____
_____
_____

9. Rabbi Ishmael

_____
_____
_____

10. Reciprocal Analogy

_____
_____
_____

11. Sanhedrin

_____
_____
_____

12. Supposition

_____
_____
_____

13. Talmud

_____
_____
_____

14. Tradition of the Elders

_____
_____
_____

15. Theology

_____
_____
_____

## Questions for Comprehension

1. Explain Paul's two conclusions in Gal 3:14.

2. What is the apparent contradiction in Gal 3:10? How does Dr. Davis attempt to resolve this dilemma?

3. What does Dunn mean when he claims that "a common assumption often underlies interpretations by viewing an antithesis between Paul and Judaism??"

4. Why have Christian scholars often concluded that the Talmud's list of midrashic methods are not relevant for New Testament study?

5. What was a likely reason for Paul's struggle to convince the Christian leaders of the midrashic conclusions he had drawn from the Hebrew Scriptures?

6. There are two implied questions that Paul is asking in Gal 3:10-13. What are these questions, and what answers did Paul disclose from Scripture through his methods of legal midrash?

# DEVELOPING BIBLE STUDY SKILLS

## What to do with a New Testament (NT) Citation of the Hebrew Scripture (HS)

Many versions of the Bible make it easy to see when a NT author cites a verse or passage from the HS; some include marginal notes while others use small capital letters. In Gal 3:10-13, Paul cites no less than four verses from Deuteronomy, Leviticus and Habakkuk. Such citations may indicate the presence of legal midrash, especially if there are two that form an analogy based on some similar word or concept. What should you do when you find a citation of the HS in the NT?

- Turn to the HS to read the verse in its context (context means the surrounding verses in which the citation is located that convey a unified thought).
- Decide whether the citation is a proof-text, or whether it is part of a midrashic argument (a proof-text merely points to a verse to "prove" some theological point).
- Return to the NT to re-read the citation in its context there.
- Consider the deeper meaning that the author is trying to convey.

*What verses in the HS constitute the context of Paul's citation of Hab 2:4? What is the narrative and theological context in which the verse appears in the HS?*

✠

*How does Paul apply Hab 2:4 to Lev 18:5? What is the implied deduction that one draws from the reciprocal analogy between these two verses? What does Paul deduce from the analogy, and why is his deduction so startling?*

✠

*What is the second deduction Paul draws from the relationship between Hab 2:4 and Lev 18:5? What is Paul's Hebraic reasoning that leads him to this deduction?*

✠

*Read Rom 4:1-25. What are the verses that Paul cites from the HS? Read each citation in its context in the HS. Are any of these citations proof-texts? Are any of the citations part of a midrashic argument from Scripture? Explain your answer. (However, do not attempt to explain the meaning of the midrash).*

✠

*Locate Mount Gerizim and Mount Ebal on an historical atlas. Then find and read the account in Scripture that narrates the twelve tribes of Israel reciting the list of curses and blessings from the two mountain peaks. Explain how Paul's citation of Deut 27:26 would have evoked this account in the minds of the Galatians.*

## Questions for Discussion

1. What is your traditional understanding of Paul's term "curse of the law" in Gal 3:10? How does your interpretation differ from the proposal in Chapter 6 of this book?

2. Why would the law fail to make you righteous? How do you become righteous in God's eyes?

3. Carefully read the citations of Deut 27:26 (in Gal 3:10) and Deut 21:23 (in Gal 3:13). How is Paul using the term "curse of the law?"

4. Now consider which of the two citations (Deut 27:26 and Deut 21:23) is the general statement of a law and which is a specific statement of that same general law? The relationship between these two verses in the HS led Paul to a new understanding about the concept of substitution. How did Paul's new understanding about substitution lead him to conclude in Gal 3:14 that God has fulfilled His promise of the Spirit?

## Application Questions

1. Yeshua kept the law perfectly, so there was no way he could be cursed by the Law. Yet Yeshua was cursed by his death on the cross. How do you explain this paradox?

2. Paul's midrash follows principles of interpretation that led to the Oral Law. In fact, this midrash would likely have become part of the Oral Law if Paul had not accepted Yeshua as the Messiah. Yet we see Yeshua keeping the law as, for example, his observation of the weekly Sabbath and the annual festivals. However, he also criticized certain parts of the Oral Law. For example, we read in Matthew that Yeshua did not require his disciples to ritually cleanse their hands before eating bread (Mat 15:2), and he performed the work of healing on the Sabbath (John 7:23). So, what should your approach be to the Oral Law?

3. How has this chapter given you a greater appreciation for what Yeshua did for both the Jews and the Gentiles?

## Digging Deeper

Do you agree with Dunn that "a common assumption often underlies interpretations by viewing an antithesis between Paul and Judaism?" Explain your answer with supporting evidence.

❧

Read the instructions about sacrifices to the Lord in Lev 1:1-7:38. Make a list of the various offerings and sacrifices with notes to describe the features of each one. Do you see a difference between those that are offerings, and those that are sacrifices? Explain the deeper metaphorical meaning of each offering/sacrifice. Which sacrifices/offerings do you think Yeshua has fulfilled? Which sacrifices/offerings do you think are still prophetic? Explain your answer.

❧

Dr. Davis asserts that, if Paul was using methods of legal midrash in the passage about "curse of the law," then perceived tensions in the passage will likely disappear. However, this can only happen if you understand the legal midrash in the passage *and* can explain it to others. Prepare an explanation and practice it in your study group. Then think of a person who might be receptive to hearing what you have to say. Deliver your explanation to this person about Paul's use of legal midrash in Galatians 3:10, 14.

# Chapter 7

## Hebraic Artistry of Language Continues:
## Believers in Christ are Sons of God

## Purpose

What is the relationship of the New Testament (NT) to the Old Testament, that is, the Hebrew Scriptures (HS)? We used to think the HS were largely a narrative background or foundation to the NT gospel of Christ. However, the more we acknowledge the abundance of citations and allusions in the NT to the HS, the more we realize how intimately connected the two testaments really are. Paul is drawing a wealth of meaning from the HS to explain accomplishments of God's Messiah, the relationship of the Messiah to those with faith in Him, and their role in God's plan for the redemption of mankind. You will continue to use a concordance to strengthen your knowledge of the HS, and to practice recognizing and fully appreciating NT citations and allusions to the HS.

## Definitions

1. *B'nei Israel*

2. *Hupo*

3. *Kal va homer*

4. Paradox

5. Seed of Abraham

6. Son of God

7.  Torah

_____

_____

_____

8.  Under the Law

_____

_____

_____

9.  *Zerah*

_____

_____

_____

_____

## Questions for Comprehension

1.  In Gal 3:15, how does Paul accomplish a sudden shift from incisive legal proof from Scripture to a dramatically new approach of persuasion?

_____

_____

_____

_____

_____

_____

_____

_____

_____

2.  How does Paul conduct a "play on words" with the Hebrew *zerah*?

_____

_____

_____

_____

_____

_____

_____

3.  In Paul's first chiastic structure in Gal 3:15-17, what is the central focus and how is it framed? How does Gal 3:18 convey a conclusion to this chiastic structure?

_____

_____

_____

_____

_____

_____

_____

_____

4. In Paul's second chiastic structure in Gal 3:19-23, what is the central focus and how is it framed? How does Gal 3:24 convey a conclusion to this chiastic structure?

5. What does Paul mean when he refers to the "promise of the Spirit"? Give specific verses and passages from the HS to support your answer.

6. What is the relationship between the law and the Spirit in Gal 3:14?

7. The nature of our inheritance is tied to two promises. According to Gal 3:29, what are these two promises? Explain your answer.

# DEVELOPING BIBLE STUDY SKILLS

### Identify Allusions to the Hebrew Scriptures (HS)

You will practice identifying allusions to the HS. Then you will use your concordance to enrich your understanding of the word, phrase or concept to which Paul is alluding.

*In Gal 3:29 Paul tells the Galatians that they are "heirs according to the promise." We remember Paul's earlier conclusion from Scripture that the Galatians have "received the promise of the Spirit by faith" (Gal 3:14). Paul seems to be referring to some promise in the HS about the Spirit. First identify the Hebrew word for Spirit. Then use your concordance to find where this Hebrew word for Spirit appears and make a list of the verses. Then browse through the list of verses that contain the word "Spirit" and select those you think are relevant. Read each in its context. How is "Spirit" used for God? How is "spirit" used when it does not refer to God?*

✝

*In Gal 3:16, Paul tells the Galatians that, when Scripture talks about the promise to Abraham and his seed, it does not mean plural seed but only one seed that is Christ. Find the specific passages in Genesis that explain God's promise to Abraham and his seed. Then use your concordance to find other passages that use the Hebrew word for "seed." Browse through the list of verses that contain the word "seed" and select those you think are relevant. Read each in its context. What are the various ways that Scripture uses the word "seed?" In Gen 1:24 God says, "Let the earth bring forth living creatures after their own kind," a concept that is connected to "seed." How do you think Paul's reference to Christ as "the seed" relates to the reproduction process?*

✝

*In Gal 3:26 (see also Gal 4:6) Paul tells the Galatians that they are sons of God. Use your concordance to find other passages that refer to sons. Browse through the list of verses that contain the word "son(s)" and select those you think are relevant. Read each in its context. What are the various ways that Scripture uses the word "son(s)?" Now return to Gal 3:26; 4:6. What would have been the response of the Galatians when they read (or heard the reading of) this part of Paul's letter?*

## Questions for Discussion

1. What has been your traditional understanding of the promised inheritance by believers in Christ? What has been your traditional understanding of the promised inheritance by the children of Israel? Is your traditional understanding beginning to change and/or broaden? If so, how? If not, explain.

2. What is the literal interpretation of Gal 3:16? Do you think the literal interpretation is compatible with the rest of Scripture? Explain.

3. What is the purpose of the law (not the Law meaning the HS but law meaning "laws")? How does Paul answer this question with irony?

4. If an angel was the mediator of the law between God and Moses, how is Yeshua now the mediator of the law between believers and God?

5. How does faith in Christ accomplish righteousness and defeat sin?

_____

_____

_____

_____

_____

_____

_____

## Application Questions

1. If you were talking with a new believer, how would you explain the relationship between the law and faith in Christ? Keep your explanation simple.

_____

_____

_____

_____

_____

_____

_____

_____

2. Revelation 3:4; 16:15 speak about garments. As a believer in Christ, how do you know if your garments are metaphorically white or not?

_____

_____

_____

_____

_____

_____

_____

_____

3. Read Mark 16:15-18, which is likely printed in red in your Bible to indicate words spoken by Yeshua. How has learning to move beyond the literal words of Scripture helped you uncover the deeper meaning of these passages in red? Demonstrate what you have learned through this passage in Mark. You should be asking questions stimulated by the text. For example, why would baptism be by the Holy Spirit and not by water? What could be the allusion to serpents in the HS? How is healing in the NT elevated beyond healing in the HS? How does the concept of salvation in v. 16 relate to the signs that will accompany those who have believed in God's son (v. 17)? What other questions might you ask? Practice answering these questions with your study group.

# *Digging Deeper*

Consider the phrase "baptized into Christ" where "baptize" is the key word. Use a concordance to find significant verses in the HS and the NT that will help you develop a full and rich understanding of this concept of cleansing. After you have finished this exercise, explain the following phrases:

- Baptized into Christ

- Clothed yourselves with Christ

- One in Christ Yeshua

Note Paul's reference to "God is One" in Gal. 3:20, and consider a possible relationship between the two phrases, "baptized into Christ" and "God is One," in the context of this passage.

❧

What do you think Yeshua meant when he said, *"Do not think that I came to abolish the Law or the Prophets; I did not come to abolish, but to fulfill"* (Mat 5:17). Before discussing the question, use your concordance to look up the Greek word that has been translated "fulfill," and read its usage in other passages to develop a full and rich understanding of this word.

❧

Explain how Scripture has shut up all men under sin.

❧

If the law was a custodian before the coming of Yeshua, what is the law now?

❧

Righteousness is a condition required of the sons of God. Find and discuss three references in the HS that demonstrate this requirement.

# Chapter 8

## The Mysterious Allegory of Hagar and Sarah

### Purpose

Paul's allegory of Hagar and Sarah is mysterious for two reasons. First, there is much dispute and discussion as to what Paul is actually trying to say in Gal 4:21-31. However, I have suggested another reason. If Paul is continuing to speak to the Galatians with Hebraic reasoning and logic in order to persuade to resist the false gospel, then his meaningless metaphors and puzzling contradictions are intentional. Paul is making the allegory "mysterious" on purpose because he expects his readers to return to the HS, not for rules of behavior but with allegorical clues and markers to help them uncover deeper meaning from Scripture. The deeper meaning is there for you also if you know how to find it.

### Definitions

1. Allegorical Marker

2. Greek Allegory

3. Greek Rhetoric

4. Metaphor

5. *Pesher*

6. Philo

7. Quintilian

8. Typology

_____

_____

_____

9. *Tupos*

_____

_____

_____

## Questions for Comprehension

1. Who is Philo? How does the evidence about allegory in Philo's writings contribute to our understanding of Paul's allegory in his letter to the Galatians? Describe this evidence.

   _____

   _____

   _____

   _____

2. Who is Quintilian? How does is the evidence about allegory in his writings contribute to our understanding of Paul's allegory in his letter to the Galatians? What is this evidence?

   _____

   _____

   _____

   _____

3. How does Paul use metaphors with no apparent meaning? Give three examples.

   _____

   _____

   _____

   _____

4. List the apparent contradictions in Gal 4:24-5:1. Explain how each is an apparent contradiction.

   _____

   _____

   _____

   _____

5. How does the location of the allegorical devices help us identify the literary structure of Paul's allegory?

   _____

   _____

   _____

   _____

6. What are various literal interpretations of Gal 4:21-5:1? Are any of the literal interpretations part of your understanding of Paul's allegory?

_____

_____

_____

_____

_____

# DEVELOPING BIBLE STUDY SKILLS

### Classical Greek Allegory and Typology

After learning how to follow Paul's artistic and legal midrash that we have seen in Gal 2:15-4:20, you were probably quite startled by Paul's "allegorically speaking." Why? Because by allegorically speaking Paul is now starting yet another method of persuasion that is different from what he has done before. Theologians have never agreed on the interpretation of Paul's allegory because they are uncertain as to the exact method he is using. This chapter has made some provocative suggestions. In order to assess these suggestions, you must first understand what has been the traditional thinking about Paul's allegory in Gal 4:21-31. That is, you must know more about classical Greek allegory and typology.

*Use the web to gain a more thorough understanding of classical Greek allegory. Discuss your findings in your study group. Then re-read Gal 4:21-31, this time explaining how some might think the passage is a classical Greek allegory. Finally, raise questions that challenge this understanding of Paul's method as Greek allegory when he says, "I speak these things allegorically."*

✝

*Use the web to gain a more thorough understanding about typology. Discuss your findings in your study group. Then re-read Gal 4:21-31. Explain how some might think that Paul was using typology in this passage. Finally, raise questions that challenge this understanding of Paul's method as typology when he says, "I speak these things allegorically."*

✝

*Summarize the suggestion of this chapter regarding the method that Paul was using in Gal 4:21-31. How does this suggestion differ from both classical Greek allegory and typology?*

✝

*Draw your own conclusion as to the method that Paul was using in Gal 4:21-31. State your conclusion as the topic sentence of a paragraph, and then build your argument by supporting your main idea with reliable and sufficient evidence.*

## Questions for Discussion

1. What is replacement theology? How has Paul's allegory contributed to this subtle perception about the way God is working with Israel?

2. List the numerous ways that Paul is contradicting Scripture when he is speaking allegorically in Gal 4:24-5:1. Do you find it disturbing that Paul is contradicting Scripture? If so, how and why do you find it disturbing? If not, why not? How is your traditional understanding of this passage interacting with Dr. Davis' suggestion that Paul is intentionally contradicting Scripture to catch our attention and to offer clues for searching in the HS?

3. The chapter began by explaining that "there is no consensus on such important topics as the main idea, the purpose for which Paul is writing this passage, and even which verses contain the conclusion." After reading the chapter, discuss your thoughts about the main idea and Paul's purpose for writing Gal 4:21-5:1.

## Application Questions

1. In John 8:34-36, Yeshua teaches about the relationship between freedom and slavery, and about being a servant or a son. How has Chapter 8, in *The Law is not a Curse,* helped you understand the ancient method of instruction that Yeshua is using in this passage?

_____
_____
_____
_____
_____
_____
_____
_____

2. How has this chapter helped you perceive the relevance of freedom and slavery in your life today? What are some of the changes that Yeshua is asking you to make?

_____
_____
_____
_____
_____
_____
_____
_____
_____

## Digging Deeper

Repeatedly Scripture narrates that a wife is barren. However, she eventually bears a child who has a great calling. Explain the examples of Sarah, Rebekah and Hannah. What is the deeper symbolic meaning of this pattern?

❧

Dr. Davis has suggested that Paul's citation of Gen 21:10, 12 has deeper symbolic significance. Discuss and explain the symbolic significance. Discuss and explain how this principal relates to your life today.

# Chapter 9

## Israel's Inheritance: Birthright of the Firstborn Son

### Purpose

Paul's allegory is mysterious, not only because of its figurative nature but also because it raises more questions than it answers. Paul apparently expected the Galatians to search the Hebrew Scriptures (HS), not for rules of behavior that shape a walk of righteousness (God's gift of the Holy Spirit has accomplished this through faith in Christ) but to follow clues and markers for deeper understanding about the nature of the inheritance. This chapter follows Paul's clues and markers to conduct such a search, which should serve as a pattern for your own search of the Scriptures.

### Definitions

1. Birthright

    _____
    _____
    _____

2. Consecration

    _____
    _____
    _____

3. *Ohn*

    _____
    _____
    _____

4. Primogeniture

    _____
    _____
    _____

5. Rashi

    _____
    _____
    _____

## Questions for Comprehension

1. Dr. Davis finds a linguistic anomaly in the shift from the singular in Ex 4:22-23 to the plural in the following narrative. What conclusions does she draw from this linguistic device?

2. One of the benefits of the birthright is a double portion of inheritance. However, this "benefit" seems to be an aid to four "responsibilities" of the birthright. What are the four responsibilities, and how does the double portion assist the son with these responsibilities?

3. How do we know from Scripture that Isaac inherited the birthright?

4. Why did Reuben lose the birthright? However, Reuben did inherit something. What was the inheritance of the tribe of Reuben?

5. Why did Esau lose the birthright?

6. Compare the special blessing that Jacob received with the blessing that his brother Esau received. How does one blessing describe the nature of the birthright, and how does the other reflect an inheritance that is not the birthright?

# DEVELOPING BIBLE STUDY SKILLS

### Following Allegorical Markers

In Paul's allegory we discovered clues that sent us to the HS for deeper meaning. These markers include the promise of a covenant, the condition of freedom and slavery, and the nature of heritage and inheritance. Dr. Davis followed the trail of inheritance and discovered the birthright. She then explored the narrative while remaining alert to any linguistic devices that point to the ancient Hebrew text. Now it is your turn. You will follow the trail of "freedom," which is the contrast to bondage. Scripture portrays the concept of "freedom" in both the Exodus event and the narrative of the wilderness wandering.

*Using your concordance, identify the various Hebrew words that convey the concepts of freedom and slavery.*

✞

*Follow the trail of bondage (that is, slavery) in the Book of Exodus by locating in your concordance all the usages of the Hebrew words for bondage or slavery and where they appear in Exodus.*

✞

*What are the causes of bondage according to Scripture? Is it possible to escape from bondage? If so, how?*

✞

*How does Scripture develop the concept of spiritual bondage? Compare spiritual bondage to physical slavery.*

✞

*Make a list of the verses in the Book of Exodus about slavery or bondage in the order in which they appear. Read each verse in its context. Now comes the hard part. You should begin to see some kind of pattern. For example, the pattern may be related to cause and effect, or you may see a contrast, or perhaps a building of some concept to its climax. These are only examples of patterns, so the pattern that emerges for you may be something different. Be prepared to present to your study group a simple description of the pattern you have seen and evidence from Scripture that supports your proposal.*

## Questions for Discussion

1. What does Paul mean when he says, "I speak these things allegorically?"

2. How does Dr. Davis see in the narrative of the HS the nature of the birthright? Give specific examples.

3. What makes Gentile believers in Christ children of promise?

4. How does "slavery" represent bondage to the ways of the world? How is it possible to know the Law and still be in bondage?

5. How does the New Testament explain how to be free from bondage to the world without knowing all the laws in the Law?

## Application Questions

1. Dr. Davis suggests that God recognizes sanctification only in the firstborn sons in order to represent a selection process whereby God is choosing those whose commitment is to obey and serve Him. Do you see an application for this in Christianity today? Explain your answer. How would you apply this principle to your own life?

2. Yeshua said, "Many are called but few are chosen." Is there an analogy to having the firstborn calling and blessing?

3. In what ways would you increase your worship of service to Yeshua?

4. How or in what ways does this chapter challenge your actions in regard to your inheritance in Yeshua?

*Digging Deeper*

In searching the HS for the nature of the inheritance known as the birthright, Dr. Davis follows a methodology that might be described as narrative and literary analysis. Explain these two forms of analysis. Then give specific examples to illustrate the various aspects of your explanation.

❧

How did Dr. Davis conclude from the HS that "all the children of Israel are born to the birthright as God's firstborn son?" Identify all of her evidence. Then relate this evidence to her conclusion. Do you agree, disagree, or agree in part but disagree in part? Explain.

❧

Compare the HS with the rest of ancient Near Eastern literature regarding the inheritance of the birthright and the redemption of the firstborn son.

❧

Compare and relate Esau's loss of the birthright with the loss of his special blessing.

# Chapter 10

## The Irony of Bondage: Only Slaves are Free

### Purpose

We will continue to follow Paul's allegorical markers, this time about the relationship of freedom and slavery to the promised inheritance. Our search will take us to the HS, as Paul was also directing the Galatians who were studying the Law. However, instead of viewing the Law as rules for right behavior, Scripture for Paul was disclosing God's plan of redemption through His Son, the Messiah. You too are learning to turn to Scripture to uncover prophetic words of promise and hope.

### Definitions

1. Barren

2. Biblical Hope

3. Circumcised Heart

4. Greek Allegory

5. Hope of Righteousness

6. Paul's Allegory

7. Pentecost

8. Tablets of Stone

## Questions for Comprehension

1. How does Paul both repeat and expand Gal 3:14 in Gal 3:29?

2. How can you learn in Scripture what Paul meant in Gal 3:14 by "the promise of the Spirit"? Be specific in your answer.

3. What are the various aspects of Spirit and spirit as Scripture explains them? Give specific examples.

4. What are the three kinds of slavery as Scripture describes them? Give specific examples both from Scripture and from your life.

5. What are the two theological aspects of each of the following concepts? One will be an aspect of the future in the form of a promise and the other will be present in our lives today.

   a. **Freedom**

      Future Promise:

      _____

      _____

      Present Reality:

      _____

      _____

   b. **Righteousness**

      Future Promise:

      _____

      _____

      Present Reality:

      _____

      _____

   c. **Sanctification**

      Future Promise:

      _____

      _____

      Present Reality:

      _____

      _____

   d. **Judgment of God's Children**

      Future Promise:

      _____

      _____

      Present Reality:

      _____

      _____

6. How does Paul use Isaiah 54:1 in his allegory?

   _____

   _____

   _____

   _____

   _____

   _____

7. How does Paul use Gen 21:10 in his allegory?

_____

_____

_____

_____

_____

_____

8. Describe the nature of true freedom as Scripture explains it.

_____

_____

_____

_____

_____

_____

_____

## DEVELOPING BIBLE STUDY SKILLS

### Irony and Word-Play in Scripture

We began our study of Galatians by learning to recognize simple literary devices that are common in Scripture such as repetition, contrast and startling insertions. We have been moving increasingly toward more complex literary techniques such as word-play and irony. Irony says one thing but really means something else. Irony sometimes results from a "play on words," so the two literary devices are often connected. Once you learn to recognize word-play and irony in Scripture, you will be surprised by how frequently these linguistic devices appear.

✝

*What is the irony of true freedom? In what way can the irony become humor? In what way can the irony be sarcastic? (Hint: humor results from laughing at yourself whereas sarcasm is directed toward others).*

✝

*Read the allegory of Hagar and Sarah in Gal 4:21-31 and give a literal interpretation. Now, re-read the passage as irony. What is ironic about Paul's discussion of the following: the covenant that Hagar represents, the present city of Jerusalem, the descendants of Hagar, the descendants of Sarah?*

## Questions for Discussion

1. Have you received the promise of the Spirit? Explain how and when. To what extent have you appropriated the promise of the Spirit in your life to better promote a walk by the Spirit?

2. Paul cites Is 54:1 in Gal 4:27. Do you see a relationship between this citation and the inheritance of the birthright? Explain.

3. Paul cites Gen 21:10 in Gal 5:30. Many have concluded that "heir" refers to eternal life, and "cast out" means loss of eternal life. What are the resulting theological conclusions to which these interpretation leads? Compare these theological conclusions with the interpretation presented by this book and the evidence on which its conclusions have been drawn.

## Application Questions

1. Explain how you have experienced the three kinds of slavery in your life. How did you respond? How would you respond today after listening to Paul in Galatians?

2. Yeshua said, *"My yoke is easy and my burden is light."* Based on what we have learned about the yoke of the law, how would you explain these words of Yeshua? How does this understanding challenge you today?

---
---
---
---
---
---
---

3. If you could paint a before and after picture of your life with the Holy Spirit, what would it look like? In other words, what has been added, and what has been shed?

---
---
---
---
---
---
---

4. Explain how slavery can be true freedom in the lordship of Christ.

---
---
---
---
---
---
---
---

## Digging Deeper

There seems to be a payment required for redemption. Explain this principle of payment for redemption in relation to the law in the HS. In the NT, how does payment for redemption apply to Yeshua? How does payment for redemption apply to all those with faith in Christ? How does payment for redemption apply selectively to those who are walking in harmony with their Lord Yeshua?

❧

Genesis 49 records Jacob's blessings of his twelve sons. Make a chart with 3 columns. List the 12 sons in the first column. Briefly identify the principle nature of each son's blessing in the second column. In the third column, list any relevant details that support the nature of the blessing.

❧

Explain how the ritual practice of sacrifice in the HS was a shadow of things to come.

# Chapter 11

## Walking by the Spirit

### Purpose

Chapter 10 addressed the last two chapters of Paul's letter to the Galatians. Paul has completed his persuasion where he used methods of artistic encouragement, legal midrash, and an ancient form of allegory. In the last two chapters of Galatians, Paul turns to those who have been convinced by his reasoning and logic. They not only believe in Yeshua the Messiah, but they are also committed to serving their Lord and Savior. Paul offers instruction, guidance and encouraging words.

### Definitions

1. *B'rit*

2. Blood Covenant

3. Cut Off

4. Fleshly Circumcision

5. Kingdom of God

6. Law of Christ

7. Mishnah

8. Natural Person

_____
_____
_____

9. Reap

_____
_____
_____

10. Spiritual Circumcision

_____
_____
_____

11. Sow

_____
_____
_____

12. *Tamim*

_____
_____
_____

## Questions for Comprehension

1. Explain how fleshly circumcision is a sign of God's covenant with His people.

_____
_____
_____
_____
_____
_____
_____

2. What is spiritual circumcision? Explain how and why spiritual circumcision is now a more elevated sign with the same principle a fleshly circumcision, but more elevated as to what it represents.

_____
_____
_____
_____
_____
_____
_____

3. What are the two aspects of fleshly circumcision and what purpose does each serve?  What are the two aspects of spiritual circumcision?

4. What are the two aspects of the Kingdom of God?

5. What is the Law of Christ and how do we fulfill it?

6. How does a Christian live as a spiritual person? What is the fruit of a spiritual person?

7. How does Scripture associate the imagery of sowing and reaping with judgment?

# DEVELOPING BIBLE STUDY SKILLS

### Patterns of Parallelism and Chiastic Structure

We have been learning to recognize the ancient literary device of chiasm throughout Paul's letter to the Galatians. Chiasm is a sophisticated form of parallelism with parallel lines on each side of a chiastic center. Parallel lines state one thing and then state it again in a way that may be similar but is often slightly different. (If it is exactly the same, the purpose of repetition would be for emphasis). Most often the second line forms an expansion, or a contrast, or there may be an intentional deletion. In each case the subtle change in the second parallel line conveys some deeper meaning. Thus, chiasm typically uses several lines of thought on one side of the central focus that relate in some way to the parallel lines on the other side. The result is a rich opportunity for depth of meaning.

*Use the web to learn more about the ancient literary device of parallelism, a poetic construction that appears throughout the books of Psalms and Proverbs. Discuss your findings in your study group.*

✝

*Use the web to learn more about the ancient literary device of chiasmus, which is found throughout Scripture. Discuss your findings in your study group.*

✝

*Review the simple chiastic pattern (A, B, A) in Gal 3:15-17 with its concluding statement in Gal 3:18. Draw a visual diagram of this chiastic pattern.*

✝

*There are often variations in the parallel patterns and chiastic structures of biblical passages. Review Gal 3:19-28 with its concluding statement in Gal 3:29. How are verses 19-20 parallel? How are verses 22-23 parallel? How do these parallel patterns form a chiastic center? How and why is the chiastic center so powerful?*

✝

*When a variation in the traditional chiastic structure appears, the ancient ear would have heard the difference and been alerted to possible deeper meaning. Review Gal 5:16-18. The chiastic structure is evident with its center in Gal 5:17b, but the pattern of parallel lines is unusual. Describe the pattern of parallel lines. What deeper meaning do you see in this unusual pattern?*

✝

*We have the same unusual chiastic construction repeated in Gal 5:18-25. What deeper meaning do you see in this unusual pattern?*

## Questions for Discussion

1. How are we living now in a spiritual war between the flesh and the Spirit? Give examples from your own experience of this spiritual warfare that relate first to an individual, then to a church, then to a denomination, and finally to a nation. What are our weapons (see Eph 6:10-18), and how do we use these weapons?

2. What kind of nervousness, concern or fear do you have about the coming judgment? What are the different ways that the loving nature of God will operate at the time of judgment? How does this understanding of God's nature mitigate your fears?

3. What Christians do you know who are living their lives as spiritual persons? Select one person and describe specific examples of visual fruit of the Spirit that the person exhibits.

4. Who do you know in your Christian community who is in a position of Christian leadership, but who is nevertheless conducting his/her life (in part or in whole) as an immature believer? How would Paul advise you to respond to this situation?

5. The imagery of sowing and reaping is portrayed as irony because a seed must die in the ground before it can produce new life. How is this irony related to the corruption of our flesh before a new life of righteousness can emerge? How is the irony also related to the death and resurrection of Yeshua?

6. Carefully consider Galatians 6:3. Then explain how pride is a form of deceit and deception.

## Application Questions

1. First explain how one walks by the Spirit. Then discuss examples from your life.

2. Do you consider yourself a servant of God? If so, why and how? How might you better serve the Lord Yeshua in His Church (see 1 Corinthians 12:1-31)?

3. Throughout this entire study of Galatians, Paul has been leading us to become a new creation by shedding the ways of the flesh and walking by the Spirit to bear fruit for God (see, in particular, Gal 6:15). You can

accomplish this by making Yeshua Lord in your life. Therefore, we suggest that you make this knowledge applicable and personal by re-reading the Gospels and noting all the words in red. In other words, what did Yeshua say that helped people walk out their lives in a way that was pleasing to God? You might want to ask him the following questions. How am I doing? What am I missing? What am I doing correctly? Who do you want me to help today?

4. Galatians 5:15 talks about the consequences of "biting and devouring one another." What have you witnessed or experienced that exhibits this kind of behavior? What were the specific consequences? What solution does Paul offer for this kind of behavior? What should be the response of the one who has experienced a severe consequence? What should be the response of one who is on the outside observing what is happening?

*Digging Deeper*

Galatians 5:10 refers to "the one who is disturbing you." To whom was Paul referring and what was the nature of the disturbance? Is the same problem evident in our world today?

⁂

In Galatians 5:11, Paul talks about those who are persecuting him. Is this the same persecution that we see in Galatians 5:10 (above) or a different kind of persecution? Is this kind of persecution still in existence today? Give some specific examples.

⁂

What does Paul mean in Galatians 6:14 when he claims that "the world has been crucified to me?"

⁂

Read the account of Aquila and Priscilla in Acts 18:18-28. A leader of the Christian community was Apollos, a powerful and charismatic personality whose heart was for the Lord Yeshua, but who nevertheless exhibited some elements of immaturity in his Christian walk. How might the actions of Apollos have caused a crisis in Ephesus? How would you describe his immaturity? (Acts does not describe the crisis Apollos would likely have precipitated, a situation similar to that in Galatia, but you can deduce the situation nevertheless). How did Aquila and Priscilla respond to this situation with Apollos in Ephesus?

www.ingramcontent.com/pod-product-compliance
Lightning Source LLC
Chambersburg PA
CBHW081220020426

42331CB00012B/3060